A Remarkable Hive

Leading with Mindfulness and Gratitude

Louis G. Spence-Smith

Mr. Remarkable

© 2025 by Louis G. Spence-Smith | Mr. Remarkable

All rights reserved. No part of this book may be reproduced, stored, or shared without written permission from the author, except for brief quotes in reviews or educational use.

www.theremarkablehive.org

info@theremarkablehive.org

Instagram: @TheRemarkableHive | YouTube: @AllThingsRemarkable

Table of Contents

DEDICATION 4

INTRODUCTION 4

Chapter 1 7

The Foundation of the Hive 7

CHAPTER 2 20

Accountability in the Hive 20

Chapter 3 29

Collaboration in the Hive 29

CHAPTER 4 37

Adaptability in the Hive 37

CHAPTER 5 46

Innovation and Growth in the Hive 46

CHAPTER 6 54

Sustainability and Balance in the Hive 54

CHAPTER 7 63

Mindfulness and Presence in the Hive 63

CHAPTER 8 72

Legacy and Impact of the Hive 72

Conclusion: 81

The Remarkable Hive 81

DEDICATION

To every leader who ever paused long enough to ask:

Am I showing up the way this moment requires?

This book is for the ones who keep asking.

INTRODUCTION

> *"As a leader, you determine the vibe. Your decisions influence the tribe. Being intentional helps the hive."*

I want to tell you something no leadership book told me.

The moment that changed how I lead didn't happen in a boardroom. It didn't happen during a strategic planning session or a performance review. It happened in a field, in front of a beehive, on a quiet morning when I had no agenda and no audience.

I was suited up — gloves, veil, smoker in hand — and I opened that hive expecting chaos. What I found was a civilization operating at a level of collective intelligence that stopped me mid-motion.

Tens of thousands of bees. No manager. No meeting. No memo. Just a shared understanding of what the hive needed — and the individual commitment to provide it. Worker bees building comb with geometric precision. Foragers returning, dancing exact coordinates to communicate where the nectar was. Guard bees reading every vibration at the entrance.

And at the center: the queen. Not commanding. Not controlling. Simply being — and through her presence, setting the entire rhythm of the colony.

I stood there a long time.

Because I recognized it. Not from nature documentaries or biology class. From every room I'd ever led in. From every team that had either come alive or slowly collapsed based on something that was harder to name than strategy or process or policy.

The vibe.

Leadership sets the tone for everything — and everything flows from that tone. The energy you carry into a room, the consistency between what you say and what you do, the way you hold yourself when the pressure is highest — these things travel. They reach people you haven't even spoken to yet. They become the culture.

This book is what I've learned — from twenty years of leading across public sector organizations, healthcare systems, and technology transformations. From the failures I had to own publicly and the breakthroughs that only came after I stopped pretending,

I had all the answers. From standing at my hives and understanding something about collective purpose that no MBA program ever taught me.

It is organized as a progression — not a checklist. Eight principles that build on each other the way a hive builds: from the foundation outward. From the individual inward.

You don't need to be a beekeeper to understand this. You just need to be someone who leads people — and who takes that responsibility seriously enough to keep growing into it.

Let's begin.

Chapter 1
The Foundation of the Hive
Setting the Tone. Building the Trust.

FROM THE HIVE

The first time I opened a hive, I expected chaos.

What I found instead was a civilization.

Tens of thousands of bees moving with complete purpose — no manager directing traffic, no meeting to align on priorities. Just a shared understanding of what the hive needed and the individual commitment to provide it. The comb built with geometric precision. The foragers dancing coordinates. The guard bees stationed and reading every vibration.

And at the center: the queen.

Not commanding. Not controlling. Simply present — and through that presence, setting the entire rhythm of the colony.

I've stood at that hive enough times now to understand something I spent years learning in conference rooms:

> The tone was already set.
> Before the first word was spoken.

Before the first decision was made.
Before anyone showed up.

The foundation was either there — or it wasn't.

> *"As a leader, you set the vibe. Your decisions shape the tribe. Lead with intention and watch it thrive."*

Leadership Starts with Intention

Leadership begins before you open your mouth.

It begins in the energy you carry into the room. The posture you hold when things are hard. The way you respond when someone brings you a problem at the worst possible moment. The consistency between what you say you value and what you actually do when no one is evaluating you.

Every team, every organization, every community has a vibe — a felt sense of what it's like to be there. Some environments feel alive: ideas move freely, people take ownership, trust is the default. Others feel like survival: guarded communication, political maneuvering, exhaustion normalized as dedication.

That difference is almost never about resources or strategy or market conditions.

It's about the foundation the leader built — or failed to build.

Intentionality is not a soft concept. It is a discipline. It means choosing — deliberately, repeatedly — how you want to show up, and then doing the work to close the gap between that intention and your actual behavior. It means being honest about the moments when you're leading from fear, from ego, from exhaustion, or from old patterns that no longer serve the people depending on you.

Leadership requires you to engage the human dimension of every decision — not the policy, not the process, not the technology. Those things matter. But they don't feel anything. The people inside your system do. And the quality of your leadership is measured not by how well you managed the process, but by what your decisions asked of the people who had to live with them.

That means deciding — again and again — whether you will be the kind of presence that generates trust or the kind that generates anxiety. Whether you will create environments where people feel safe to be honest, or environments where people learn to perform safety while hiding their real experience.

The questions that anchor intentional leadership are not complicated:

- → How do I want people to feel when they work with me?
- → What do I want my team to be able to say about this environment a year from now?
- → Am I being the leader today that the work — and the people — actually require?

Simple questions. Uncomfortable to answer honestly.

Worth asking every day.

A Personal Story: Setting the Vibe

I walked into a hive that had forgotten what it felt like to function.

Not my beehive — though I've walked into struggling ones of those too. I mean an organization. A team. A place where the collective weight of unaddressed dysfunction had settled into the walls and the silences and the way people didn't quite meet your eyes in the hallway.

Morale was low. Processes were undefined. Burnout was the operating environment, not the exception. Some people were disengaged — not because they didn't care, but because caring had cost them something in the past and they'd stopped being willing to pay. Others were confused: uncertain of their roles, unsure of what success looked like, showing up but not sure why.

I felt the vibe the moment I arrived.

It wasn't chaos — chaos would have been easier to work with. It was something more stubborn. It was resignation.

My first instinct — the one that comes from years of being trained to produce results and demonstrate competence — was to move quickly. Identify the problems. Implement solutions. Show momentum. Justify my presence.

I didn't.

Instead, I went quiet. I observed. I asked questions I had no agenda attached to. I paid attention not just to what people said but to what they didn't say — where they hesitated, where they deflected, where the careful language was doing the work of protecting something fragile underneath.

I was reading the hive.

What I found was a team that had been led by authority without trust. Direction without transparency. Accountability without support. People had learned that the safest move was to stay small, stay quiet, and wait for instructions. Initiative had been punished often enough that no one tried it anymore.

So, I started with consistency. I showed up the same way every day. I said what I meant. I followed through on what I said I would do — even the small things, especially the small things, because small things are how people decide whether the big things can be trusted. I made space for people to voice concerns without those concerns being used against them. I took ownership publicly when I got something wrong.

It took time. Trust always does.

But slowly — the way a hive recalibrates when a new queen is introduced, gradually and then all at once — the vibe shifted. People started bringing ideas. Conversations got more honest. The energy that had been spent on self-protection started flowing toward the actual work.

That experience confirmed something I had sensed but hadn't fully articulated:

> The energy you bring is contagious.
> The standard you hold — for yourself first — becomes the standard.
> The culture you want from your team begins in how you show up when it's hardest to.

> *The hive doesn't thrive on good intentions. It thrives on what actually gets done.*

The Hive Model of Leadership

The hive doesn't run on inspiration alone. It runs on three integrated principles that reinforce each other — and when one breaks down, the whole system feels it.

1. **Structure — Clarity as a Form of Respect**

    Every bee knows its role — not because someone told it this morning, but because the system is designed for that knowledge to exist. In leadership, structure is how you make clarity accessible. When people know what success looks like, what they're responsible for, and how their work connects to the larger purpose — they can operate with confidence. Confusion isn't a personality trait. It's usually a structural failure.

2. **Flexibility — The Permission to Adapt**

    The hive doesn't collapse when conditions change. Foragers shift to new sources. Roles flex based on what the colony needs. Structure gives the foundation; flexibility is what makes the structure durable. Leaders who only know how to hold the plan eventually hold it past the point where it's serving anyone. The leaders who last know when to pivot without abandoning the purpose behind the plan.

3. **Accountability — Ownership Without Fear**

    In the hive, accountability is not enforced through surveillance. It emerges from shared stakes. Every bee understands that its contribution matters to the survival of the whole. When leaders create that same sense of shared stakes — when team members understand that their effort is meaningful and their ownership is real — accountability becomes intrinsic. It stops being something you demand and becomes something people bring.

These three principles are not sequential. They exist simultaneously. You can't build accountability in a team that has no structural clarity. You can't sustain flexibility in a team with no foundation of trust. They feed each other — and your job is to tend to all three.

The Ripple Effect of Leadership

Leadership is not contained to the moments when you're actively leading.

It lives in the story your team tells about you when you're not in the room. It lives in whether people feel safer or more anxious when you walk in. It lives in whether the people who work with you are growing — or contracting — in response to the environment you've created.

A hive where the queen is struggling doesn't just produce less honey. It becomes vulnerable — to disease, to collapse, to losing the collective capacity it needs to survive. The stakes are that real.

Leadership that is merely adequate has a cost. Leadership that is disengaged, inconsistent, or self-protective has a larger one. The ripple moves outward whether you intend it to or not.

The only question is what kind of ripple you're creating.

> *"You determine the vibe. Your decisions influence the tribe. Being intentional helps the hive."*

Key Takeaways

1. **You are the signal your team reads.**
   Before strategy, before process — your presence, consistency, and energy establish what kind of environment this is.

2. **Intention is a daily practice, not a declaration.**
   Deciding who you want to be as a leader is the beginning. Closing the gap between that decision and your actual behavior is the ongoing work.

3. **Structure, flexibility, and accountability are interdependent.**
   Tend to all three. Neglecting one weakens the others.

4. **Trust is built in small moments — and lost in them too.**
   Consistency in the ordinary is what makes you credible in the extraordinary.

Your Challenge

This week, don't ask your team what they need. Ask yourself:

- → What is the actual vibe of my environment right now — and how much of it did I create?
- → Where is there a gap between the leader I intend to be and the leader I've been showing up as?
- → What is one thing I can do consistently this week — not once, but every day — that demonstrates the standard I want to set?

Write it down. Not as a goal. As a commitment.

CHAPTER 2
Accountability in the Hive
Own Your Role. Own Your Impact.

FROM THE HIVE

A hive never produces honey by accident.

Every forager that returns with nectar has flown a specific route, visited specific flowers, and made dozens of micro-decisions about where to go and when to return. And when she gets back, she doesn't simply drop the nectar and disappear. She dances — literally — communicating exactly where the resource is so others can find it. She takes ownership of the information. She closes the loop.

No one forced her to dance. No one audited her flight path. She does it because the hive depends on it — and she knows it.

That is accountability in its most honest form.

Not a policy. Not a performance review. A lived understanding that your contribution is load-bearing.

> *"Accountability is the bridge between intention and impact."*

What Accountability Actually Is

Accountability is one of the most misused words in leadership.

In most organizations it arrives as a warning. It shows up in post-mortems and disciplinary processes. It gets invoked when something has gone wrong and someone needs to be identified. It functions, in practice, as a synonym for blame.

That is not accountability. That is consequence management with a better-sounding name.

Real accountability is prospective, not retrospective. It means owning your role before the outcome arrives — not just after it goes wrong. It means being clear about what you said you would do, honest about whether you did it, and willing to examine your own contribution to whatever unfolded. Including — especially — the contribution of your inaction.

Accountability starts with you.

As a leader, your ability to take ownership of your decisions — the ones that worked and the ones that didn't — sets the entire standard for your team. Not your policy documents. Not your stated values. Your behavior in the moment when owning something is uncomfortable.

If you model transparency, your team will follow. If you deflect, they'll learn to deflect. The hive takes its cues from the center.

A Personal Story: Owning My 50%

There was a period in my leadership when progress stalled — and I couldn't figure out why.

I had implemented what I believed were the right strategies. The plan was sound. The intentions were clear. But the team was struggling — inefficiencies compounding, burnout spreading, alignment slipping. We were moving, but we weren't moving together.

My first instinct was to look outward. The constraints were real. The environment was difficult. There were factors genuinely beyond my control, and it was tempting to rest my case there.

But I had a practice — one I'd developed over years of leading through hard situations — of asking myself a single question when things weren't working:

"What's my 50%?"

Not what went wrong. Not who fell short. My 50. The portion of this outcome that my decisions, my behaviors, my silence, or my assumptions helped create.

When I sat with that question honestly, the answers were uncomfortable.

I had set expectations I thought were clear — but hadn't checked for understanding. I had communicated a vision that made sense to me — but hadn't translated it into language the team could act on. I had been present in the work — but absent in the moments when people needed me to slow down, listen, and recalibrate.

So I owned it. Publicly, with the team. Not as a performance of humility, but as a genuine reset.

I acknowledged what wasn't working. I shared what I was going to do differently. I invited them to tell me what I was missing — and then I actually listened to what they said.

The shift that followed wasn't immediate. But it was real. When a leader owns their role in a problem, it gives the team permission to own theirs. Accountability became something we practiced together instead of something I demanded from above.

That experience taught me something I return to constantly:

> Leadership isn't about having the right answers.
> It's about asking the right questions —
> starting with the ones pointed at yourself.

Building a Culture of Accountability

Culture is not what you write on the wall. It is the sum of what you tolerate, what you celebrate, and what you model every day.

A culture of accountability doesn't emerge from stricter oversight or more detailed reporting. It emerges when people understand that ownership is safe — that taking responsibility for their work won't be weaponized against them, that raising a problem is valued more than hiding one, that the goal is progress, not punishment.

Here's how you build it:

1. **Set expectations with clarity, not assumption.**
   Accountability can't exist where expectations are vague. Be specific about what success looks like, who owns what, and what done means. Then check for understanding — not just compliance. A nod in a meeting is not confirmation.

2. **Model ownership before you require it.**
   If you want your team to own their mistakes, own yours first. If you want them to raise problems early, be someone who responds to early problems with curiosity, not blame. You are demonstrating the terms of accountability every time you respond to difficulty.

3. **Separate accountability from punishment.**
   When accountability is experienced as a precursor to consequences, people stop being honest. Create

the conditions where owning a problem is the path to solving it — not the path to a performance improvement plan.

4. **Celebrate ownership in action.**
When someone steps up, names a gap, takes responsibility without being asked — acknowledge it. Specifically, publicly when appropriate. What gets recognized gets repeated.

The hive doesn't need a manager watching every bee. The system works because every bee understands its stakes. Build the same understanding in your team — and accountability becomes something the culture carries, not something you have to chase.

The Ripple Effect of Accountability

When leaders own their role — genuinely, not performatively — something moves in the team.

People begin to bring problems earlier, before they compound. They stop spending energy managing impressions and start spending it on the actual work. Trust deepens, because everyone can see that honesty is safe here. Progress accelerates, because the team is working with reality instead of around it.

Accountability isn't a burden. It's a bridge. Between what you said you'd do and what you actually did. Between the leader you intend to be and the one your team experiences. Between the environment you want and the one you're actually building.

Cross that bridge consistently — and the hive will follow.

The hive is built on honest contribution. Your leadership is too.

Key Takeaways

1. **Accountability is prospective, not just retrospective.**
   Own your role before the outcome arrives — not only after it goes wrong.

2. **Ask yourself: What's my 50%?**
   In any breakdown, examine your own contribution honestly before looking outward.

3. **Culture is what you model, not what you mandate.**
   The terms of accountability are set by how you respond when ownership is hard.

4. **Separate accountability from consequence.**
   When owning a problem feels safe, people stop hiding problems. That is when teams start winning.

Your Challenge

This week, identify one situation — current or recent — where something didn't go the way you intended.

Don't start with what went wrong externally. Start with:

- → What was my 50% in this outcome?
- → Where was I unclear, absent, or avoidant when the situation needed something different from me?
- → What would it look like to own that — with my team, not just in my journal?

Then do it. Say it out loud. Watch what shifts.

Chapter 3
Collaboration in the Hive
No Single Bee Builds the Hive Alone.

FROM THE HIVE

There is a moment inside every thriving hive that stops me every time I witness it.

A forager returns. She has found something — a rich source of nectar, far from the hive. And instead of keeping that information, she shares it. Through a precise sequence of movement, angle, and duration — what biologists call the waggle dance — she communicates the exact location. Distance. Direction relative to the sun. Quality of the source.

She doesn't protect the information. She broadcasts it.

Because in the hive, hoarding is a threat to survival. Sharing is how the colony thrives.

I've thought about that dance in rooms where people were protecting information like it was personal currency. Where silos were maintained because knowledge meant leverage. Where collaboration was the word on the poster and competition was the actual operating system.

That is not a hive. That is a collection of bees living in proximity.

The difference is intention.

> *"Collaboration is the key to transforming ideas into impact. When the hive works together, it thrives."*

What Collaboration Actually Requires

Collaboration is not consensus. It is not everyone agreeing or everyone being comfortable. It is not the absence of tension.

Real collaboration is the willingness to bring your full capability into a shared space — and to trust that others will do the same. It requires a foundation of psychological safety, where people can speak honestly without the fear that honesty will cost them something. It requires leaders who know when to direct and when to step back. And it requires a clarity of purpose strong enough to hold the group together when individual perspectives pull in different directions.

Collaboration doesn't just happen. It must be designed, nurtured, and led.

Your job as a leader is not to be the most collaborative person in the room. It is to create the conditions where collaboration becomes the natural behavior of the room.

A Personal Story: Building Collaboration in Uncertain Times

I stepped into a team that had forgotten how to work together.

This was the Mid-Atlantic. A leadership environment defined by fragmentation, political transitions, and the particular kind of institutional fatigue that sets in when an organization has reorganized one too many times without ever addressing what was actually broken. The team was siloed by design — each group protecting its lane, its information, its position. Disengagement wasn't apathy. It was self-preservation.

I was the newcomer. And I had no mandate to restructure, no authority to realign, and no budget for anything dramatic. What I had was time, attention, and a commitment to going slow enough to actually understand what I was dealing with before I tried to change it.

The first thing I looked for was the foragers — the people who were still dancing. Still willing to share what they knew. Still capable of being curious about solutions rather than calcified in their grievances. They existed. They always do. And they became my starting point.

I built around them — not over the skeptics, but toward them. I established office hours: no agenda, no performance, just space for people to bring whatever they were carrying. I introduced Agile sprints not as a methodology lecture but as a practical offer: let's try something for two weeks and see what we learn. I created pseudo-Scrum Master roles — informal leadership opportunities for people who had been overlooked for the formal ones.

I listened more than I spoke. Not as a technique — as a genuine orientation. I needed to understand the terrain before I could navigate it. And the terrain was people: their frustrations, their histories with leadership, their quiet hopes that this time might be different.

Slowly, the culture shifted. Not dramatically — there was no single moment of transformation. It was incremental. One honest conversation. One shared problem. One instance of a team member bringing an idea and having it received well enough to bring another one.

By the time collaboration had become visible, it had already been building underground for months.

That experience confirmed something I believe deeply:

> Collaboration is not built in the launch moment.
> It is built in the listening moment.
> The consistency moment.
> The moment you prove that sharing is safe.

Creating the Conditions for Collaboration

1. Start with a shared vision — not a shared task.

Collaboration aligns around purpose, not just process. When people understand why the work matters and how their role connects to the larger outcome, they have a reason to work across their own boundaries. Without that clarity, collaboration is just coordination.

2. Build trust through transparency — consistently, not occasionally.

People collaborate in proportion to how much they trust the environment. Transparency is not a one-time announcement — it's a practice. What you share about challenges, what you admit when you don't know something, what you do when you receive difficult feedback — these build the ground collaboration requires.

3. Create structured space for cross-boundary work.

Collaboration doesn't emerge from good intentions alone. It needs design. Regular cross-functional touchpoints. Clear handoff protocols. Forums where different parts of the team can see each other's work. The structure doesn't constrain collaboration — it enables it.

4. **Remove the blockers, not just the tasks.**

   The most effective thing a leader can do for collaboration is identify and eliminate what's making it hard. Unclear ownership. Competing incentives. Information hoarding. Legacy rivalries. These are the invisible walls. Name them. Address them.

5. **Welcome the friction.**

   Healthy collaboration includes disagreement. Managed well, tension between perspectives produces better outcomes than false harmony. Your role is not to eliminate conflict — it is to create a container where conflict generates insight instead of damage.

The Ripple Effect of Collaboration

When collaboration becomes the culture — not the aspiration but the actual operating reality — something measurable shifts.

Problems get solved faster because the people who have the relevant information are actually talking to each other. Ideas improve because they get stress-tested before they get implemented. People feel more ownership over outcomes because they contributed to creating them.

Resilience grows because the team is no longer dependent on any single person's knowledge or presence.

And perhaps most importantly: people want to be there. When work feels like genuine contribution toward something shared, it becomes meaningful in a way that no individual success can replicate.

The forager dances because the hive depends on it.

Build a team where people feel that same truth — and watch what becomes possible.

The hive doesn't coordinate by memo. It coordinates through trust, shared stakes, and the willingness to dance.

Key Takeaways

1. **Collaboration is designed, not wished for.**
   Create the conditions — the structure, the safety, the shared purpose — and collaboration follows.

2. **Find your foragers.**
   Every team has people still willing to share, to build, to lead. Start there.

3. **Transparency is the infrastructure of trust.**
   What you share, when you share it, and how you receive what others share — this is how trust is built or burned.

4. **Friction is not failure.**
   Healthy disagreement, managed intentionally, strengthens the outcome. Protect the space for honest tension.

Your Challenge

This week, look at your team with honest eyes:

- → Where are the silos? What's maintaining them — culture, incentive, unaddressed history?
- → Who are your foragers — the ones still willing to share and build? Are you giving them visible space to do that?
- → What is one structural change you could make — not a conversation, but a system — that would make collaboration easier?

Don't announce a collaboration initiative. Create one condition that makes collaboration more possible.

CHAPTER 4
Adaptability in the Hive
Pivot with Purpose. Thrive Through Change.

FROM THE HIVE

In late summer, the hive begins to prepare for winter.

Not because anyone announces it. Not because there's a planning meeting or a seasonal strategy document. The bees sense the shift — in temperature, in daylight, in the diminishing return of foraging flights — and they begin to adapt. Drones are expelled. Winter bees are raised. The cluster forms. Resources are conserved with a precision that has nothing to do with policy and everything to do with survival.

The hive doesn't mourn summer. It moves.

I've thought about that transition often — standing at my hives in August, watching the colony begin its invisible reconfiguration — and I've thought about all the leaders I've seen who couldn't do what the bees do instinctively: read the moment honestly, release what no longer serves, and reorganize around what the new reality actually requires.

Adaptability isn't a skill you develop in calm conditions. It's a discipline you build before you need it.

> *"It's not the strongest or the most intelligent who thrive, but those most adaptable to change."*

The Power to Pivot

In leadership, you will not always control what happens. Budgets tighten. Priorities shift. People leave. The landscape changes in ways no plan fully anticipated. The difference between leaders who sustain momentum and those who lose it is rarely about what happened to them. It's about how quickly and honestly they engaged with the new reality.

Adaptability is not abandoning your direction. It is being honest enough to recognize when the path to that direction needs to change.

Leaders who cling to plans past their usefulness are not being disciplined. They are confusing commitment to a destination with attachment to a route. The destination matters. The route is a tool. Tools get updated.

What makes this hard is that changing course — especially publicly — can feel like admitting failure. It can feel like weakness. But in reality, the willingness to pivot when conditions demand it is one of the clearest demonstrations of leadership maturity. It communicates that you are paying attention, that you are honest, and that the mission matters more than being right about the method.

That is what your team is watching for.

A Personal Story: Navigating Change and Earning Trust

I've stepped into versions of the same situation more than once: a team in transition, operating in an environment of uncertainty, led by someone new — me — whose credibility was still unproven.

The most instructive version came during one of my most challenging leadership assignments. The team was burnt out. The organization's roadmap was unclear. Priorities had been shifting without adequate explanation, and the staff had learned to be skeptical — of new leadership in particular — because new leadership had historically meant new chaos.

I couldn't arrive with a plan. The plan would have been fiction. I didn't yet know enough about the terrain to make commitments I could keep.

So instead, I arrived with a question: What do we actually have to work with?

I did a real inventory. Not of what we were supposed to have, but of what was actually there — systems, capabilities, people, existing momentum, even small wins no one had named. From that honest baseline, I built a 30-60-90 day framework: not a grand vision, but achievable milestones. Small enough to deliver on. Clear enough to communicate. Honest enough that people could see whether we were doing what we said we'd do.

I introduced sprints — short cycles of focused work with clear outputs — borrowed from Agile practice, adapted for the context. The point wasn't the methodology. The point was momentum. Small wins, compounded, begin to change what a team believes is possible.

Transparency was non-negotiable. When something wasn't working, I said so. When I needed to change direction, I explained why — not as a justification for my authority, but as a genuine communication to people who deserved to understand the reasoning behind decisions that affected their work.

What I earned — slowly, through consistency — was trust. Not charisma-based trust. Evidence-based trust. The kind that forms when people can observe that you do what you say, that you tell the truth about what's hard, and that you're willing to adjust when adjusting is what the situation needs.

The team adapted. Not because I mandated adaptation, but because I modeled it — and made it safe enough to try.

Resilience: The Other Side of Adaptability

Adaptability and resilience are not the same thing — but they are inseparable.

Adaptability is about changing what you do. Resilience is about maintaining who you are while you do it. It's the quality that allows you to absorb difficulty — a failed initiative, a lost relationship, a setback that felt avoidable — and emerge from it still oriented toward your purpose.

Resilient leaders don't pretend challenges aren't hard. They don't perform positivity over genuine difficulty. What they do is refuse to let the difficulty become the final story. They stay curious about what the setback is teaching. They look for the adjustment it's calling for. And they model that orientation for the people around them — demonstrating that progress doesn't require a straight line, only a persistent direction.

In the hive, the colony doesn't collapse when foragers return empty-handed. It recalibrates. It sends different scouts. It adjusts its assessment of where the resources are. The resilience is in the system, not in the performance of any single bee.

Your resilience, as a leader, eventually becomes part of the system your team operates in. Build it deliberately.

Key Principles for Adaptability and Resilience

1. **Stay anchored to the outcome, not the plan.**
   When conditions change, revisit your goals — not to abandon them, but to ask: is the current path still the most honest route to where we're going? If not, change the path.

2. **Make change legible.**
   People don't resist change as much as they resist unexplained change. When you pivot, communicate the reasoning. Not as a defense, but as a genuine orientation — so the team can adapt with you instead of reacting to you.

3. **Break transformation into increments.**
   Large-scale change overwhelms. Small, visible progress builds the confidence and momentum that makes larger change possible. Use short cycles. Celebrate small wins. Let the team see that adaptation is working.

4. **Model resilience in the difficult moments, not just the easy ones.**

How you respond to a failed initiative, a public setback, or a decision that didn't land — that is the resilience lesson your team will carry. Approach it with honesty, curiosity, and forward orientation.

5. **Equip your team to adapt without you.**

    The goal is not a team that follows you through change. It's a team that has internalized the capacity for change — so that when you're not there, they can still move.

Key Takeaways

1. **Adaptability is commitment to the destination, not the route.**
   Change the path when the path stops serving the purpose.

2. **Transparency transforms pivots.**
   Unexplained change breeds anxiety. Explained change builds alignment.

3. **Resilience is a system, not a personality trait.**
   Build it into how your team operates — not just how you perform.

4. **Small wins compound.**
   Break change into visible increments. What the team can see, the team can trust.

Your Challenge

This week, identify one place where you or your team are holding on to something past its usefulness — a strategy, a process, an assumption — because changing it feels like losing.

- → What would an honest assessment of current conditions tell you about this?
- → What would it look like to adapt — not abandon, but adapt — with intention?
- → How would you communicate that change in a way that brings your team with you rather than leaving them to guess?

The hive doesn't mourn summer. It moves.

Adapt. Not because the mission changed. Because the path to it requires honesty.

CHAPTER 5
Innovation and Growth in the Hive

Think Beyond the Obvious. Lead Beyond the Expected.

FROM THE HIVE

When a hive runs out of space, it doesn't wait to be told what to do.

It swarms.

Half the colony, led by the old queen, leaves to find a new home. The remaining bees raise a new queen and rebuild. What looks from the outside like disruption — thousands of bees suddenly in the air, the hive apparently splitting — is actually one of the most sophisticated acts of distributed innovation in nature. The colony solves a resource problem by dividing its capacity and expanding its reach. Neither half collapses. Both grow.

Innovation, when it is real, often looks like that. Not polished. Not predictable. A willingness to break from what has always worked in order to solve for what the current reality actually requires.

Most organizations wait too long to swarm. They optimize within existing constraints until the constraints become the identity — and then wonder why nothing new is possible.

> *"In times of change, leaders innovate. In times of uncertainty, leaders pivot. Progress requires both."*

What Innovation Actually Demands

Innovation in leadership is not about grand gestures or disruptive vision statements. It is about creating an environment where the people closest to the work feel safe and empowered to question how the work is done — and where experimentation is treated as intelligence-gathering rather than risk.

Most of the barriers to innovation in organizations are not technical. They are cultural. People have ideas. They have seen inefficiencies, spotted opportunities, and imagined better approaches. What stops them from bringing those ideas forward is their assessment of the likely response.

Will this be taken seriously? Will I be protected if it doesn't work? Is the stated appetite for innovation matched by actual behavior at the top?

As a leader, your job is to answer those questions — through your behavior, not your communication strategy — in a way that makes the honest answer yes.

A Personal Story: Innovating Under Constraints

The assignment looked, on paper, like it was designed to prevent innovation.

Severe resource constraints. Staff stretched thin across competing priorities. A budget that had been cut enough times to make ambition feel irresponsible. A timeline that left no room for the kind of reflection that meaningful change requires.

I've learned that these are precisely the conditions where innovation either emerges or disappears permanently — because constraint forces honesty. You can't rely on resources you don't have. You can't defer to processes that aren't working. You have to look at what's actually there and ask what it's actually capable of.

So I started by listening and looking.

Not at the gaps — I already knew the gaps. I looked at the existing capabilities the team hadn't fully used. The tools already in place that no one had configured optimally. The institutional knowledge that lived in specific people and had never been systematized. The small workarounds individuals had developed that, scaled, could become actual solutions.

I engaged the team in that inventory. Brought them into the assessment. Asked them where they saw friction, where they saw opportunity, where they'd thought about doing something differently but hadn't had the space to try. Their answers were the innovation. I didn't have to invent anything. I had to create the conditions where what they already knew could surface.

We introduced pilot projects — small-scale tests of new approaches before committing fully. Short sprint cycles that let us learn without overcommitting. A norm of naming what we learned from both the pilots that worked and the ones that didn't.

Over time, the team's relationship to constraints shifted. The limitations were still real. But they had stopped being the final word. Innovation, we discovered, is not the absence of constraints. It's the refusal to let them become an identity.

The Leader's Role in Innovation

1. **Create safety for creative risk.**
   Innovation requires people to try things that might not work. If trying something that doesn't work leads to punishment, people stop trying. Build a culture where a well-reasoned experiment that fails is a contribution — not a liability.

2. **Model agility.**

   When your own strategy isn't working, pivot visibly and explain your reasoning. Your team is watching whether adaptation is something you require of them or something you practice yourself.

3. **Empower problem-ownership.**

   Innovative leaders don't solve every problem themselves — they give problems to the people who are closest to them and have the most relevant knowledge. Then they protect the space for those people to work.

4. **Balance speed and thoughtfulness.**

   Agility does not mean urgency in all directions at once. It means moving quickly on what you know, and pausing deliberately to learn what you don't. Sprint cycles are a tool for this — small, focused, iterative.

5. **Foster a growth orientation.**

   Every setback contains information. Leaders who respond to difficulty with curiosity — What did this teach us? What do we adjust? — build teams that learn continuously rather than teams that protect themselves from failure.

The Ripple Effect of Innovative Leadership

When innovation becomes part of the culture — not an initiative but a way of operating — the organization gains something that no single strategy can provide: the capacity to solve problems that haven't happened yet.

Teams that have learned to experiment, to learn, to pivot with intention — these teams are not just more productive.

They are more resilient. They can absorb change because they've been practicing change. They can face uncertainty because they've been trained, through experience, that uncertainty is where good thinking happens.

The hive swarms not because it wants disruption but because it has outgrown its current form. Growth required it.

Lead in a way that your team outgrows what's currently possible — and is ready for what comes next.

Key Takeaways

1. **Innovation is cultural before it is technical.**
   Build the conditions — safety, empowerment, honest feedback — and the ideas will come.

2. **Constraints force clarity.**
   The absence of resources is often the beginning of real creativity. Engage with what's there.

3. **Small experiments produce large learning.**
   Pilot projects and sprint cycles are not compromises — they are how sophisticated organizations learn.

4. **Your response to failure sets the standard.**
   How you receive a well-intentioned experiment that didn't work tells the team everything about whether to try again.

Your Challenge

This week, identify one area where your team has been working around a problem rather than solving it:

- → What is one small experiment — a two-week pilot, a process test, a new approach to a familiar problem — that could generate real learning?
- → Who on your team has an idea they haven't fully brought forward? What would it take to create the space for them to try it?
- → How do you currently respond when something doesn't work? What does that response signal to your team about whether it's safe to try?

Don't wait for the perfect conditions. The hive doesn't wait for perfect weather to swarm.

Innovation is not a moment. It is a practice. Start the practice.

CHAPTER 6
Sustainability and Balance in the Hive
Build for Longevity. Lead Beyond Your Tenure.

FROM THE HIVE

A beehive in winter looks like it has stopped.

From the outside, there is almost no activity. The entrance is quiet. The foraging has ceased. A casual observer might conclude the colony is dormant — resting, waiting, surviving.

What's actually happening is remarkable.

The bees have formed a winter cluster — a living sphere of tens of thousands of bees generating heat through constant muscle movement. The bees on the outside rotate inward before they get too cold. The ones inside rotate outward to take their turn at the perimeter. The cluster breathes as one organism, sustained by the honey they spent all summer storing. No individual bee survives the winter alone. The cluster does.

Sustainability in the hive is not about individual heroics. It is about designing a system that can function — that can self-regulate — even when conditions are hostile and resources are scarce.

Leadership is no different.

> *"True leadership is not about leaving your mark — it's about leaving a legacy that endures."*

What Sustainable Leadership Actually Means

The most common mistake leaders make with sustainability is treating it as a future concern. Something to think about at the end of a tenure, before a transition, when the work is mature enough to document.

By then, it's usually too late to build it properly.

Sustainable leadership is not a phase — it's an orientation. It means making decisions from the beginning that consider what you're leaving behind, not just what you're building right now. It means developing people rather than just utilizing them. Building processes that are documented and transferable rather than living exclusively in your own institutional knowledge. Creating accountability structures that function when you're not there to enforce them.

It also means taking care of yourself.

A leader who is burning out cannot build a sustainable team. You cannot pour from empty — and no strategic framework compensates for a leader whose own reserves are depleted. Sustainability begins with the discipline to protect your own capacity: to rest, to reflect, to maintain the practices that keep you thinking clearly and showing up fully.

The winter cluster survives because no single bee is required to do more than it can. The system is designed for shared load. Your leadership system should be too.

A Personal Story: Building Sustainable Teams

The systems were outdated. The staff were stretched thin. Burnout had moved from exception to operating environment, and there was a lack of accountability, structure, and direction that had compounded over time until it had become the culture.

When I stepped into that role, the temptation — as it always is in environments of visible disorder — was to act. To restructure, to impose, to demonstrate competence through velocity. To show that a leader had arrived.

Instead, I started with an inventory.

Not a performance review or a gap analysis — an honest accounting of what was actually there. What systems existed, even if they were underused. What knowledge lived in which people. What small sources of momentum were already present, however quiet. What the team could build on before I introduced anything new.

From that inventory, I built in phases. Thirty days to understand and stabilize. Sixty days to begin improving. Ninety days to start building toward something durable. At each phase, I communicated clearly what we were doing and why. I created visible markers of progress so the team could see that change was real and directional — not just another reorganization that would dissolve into the next one.

I empowered individuals into leadership roles — not as a management strategy but as a genuine investment. I identified people whose potential hadn't been recognized and gave them real responsibility. I made clear that these weren't temporary assignments — they were part of a design for a team that could function beyond any single person's presence, including mine.

I also brought my own practices into the work: mindfulness, reflection, the daily habit of gratitude. Not as a wellness program — as a demonstration. A leader who models those habits signals that the pace of the work doesn't have to consume the person doing it.

By the time I transitioned out, the team had something they hadn't had when I arrived: a foundation that didn't depend on me. The systems were documented. The leadership was distributed. The culture of continuous improvement was embedded in the rhythm of how they worked.

That is the measure I hold myself to:

> Not what I built.
> What they were able to build after I left.

The Three Pillars of Sustainable Leadership

1. **Empowerment — Build People, Not Dependency.**

   Sustainable leaders invest in the development of others as a primary function of their role — not a secondary one. They delegate not just tasks but authority and ownership. They create opportunities for team members to lead, fail, learn, and grow. A team that depends entirely on a single leader is not a sustainable system — it is a single point of failure.

2. **Resilient Systems — Build for When You're Not There.**

   Documented processes. Clear ownership. Shared knowledge. These are not bureaucratic overhead — they are the infrastructure of sustainability. A system that runs because everyone knows what to do, not because a specific person is there to direct it every day, is a system that can survive leadership transitions, unexpected absences, and growth.

3. **Continuous Improvement — Build a Culture That Learns.**

   Sustainable teams don't optimize for the current state — they build in the mechanisms for ongoing refinement. Regular retrospectives. Honest feedback loops. A norm of naming what's working and what isn't before problems compound into crises. Learning, institutionalized, is what keeps a system from calcifying.

The Ripple Effect of Sustainable Leadership

The leaders who built something that outlasted them rarely talked about sustainability as a philosophy. They just kept asking a question:

If I weren't here tomorrow, what would this team need?

And then they built it — quietly, consistently, over time.

That is the ripple effect of sustainable leadership. It isn't visible in quarterly results. It shows up years later, in teams that still function with purpose, in leaders who were developed under you and now develop others, in systems that absorbed change without collapsing.

The hive stores honey all summer for a winter it hasn't experienced yet.

Build your team the same way.

Key Takeaways

1. **Sustainability is an orientation, not a phase.**
   Build for longevity from the beginning — not when the transition is imminent.

2. **Empower others to lead.**
   A team that depends entirely on you is a team at risk. Distribute leadership intentionally.

3. **Systems outlast individuals.**
   Documentation, shared ownership, and continuous improvement are the infrastructure of lasting impact.

4. **Sustainability starts with you.**
   A leader who is burning out cannot build a sustainable team. Protect your own capacity.

Your Challenge

This week, ask yourself one honest question:

If I weren't here tomorrow — what would this team need that they don't currently have?

- → What knowledge lives only in your head that should be documented and shared?
- → Who on your team is ready for more responsibility — and what's stopping you from giving it to them?
- → What practice — for yourself, not just the team — are you neglecting that you know you need to sustain your own leadership?

Build one thing this week that will still be standing after you've moved on.

The winter cluster survives because the system was built for winter long before winter arrived.

CHAPTER 7
Mindfulness and Presence in the Hive
Be Here. Lead from Here.

FROM THE HIVE

There is a sound inside a healthy hive that you can only hear when you're still.

It's not the buzzing of individual bees. It's something more unified than that — a collective hum that sounds almost like a chord. Beekeepers learn to listen for it. It tells you, before you see anything, what kind of hive you're entering. A distressed hive sounds different. An agitated hive sounds different. A Queenless hive sounds different.

Presence is the prerequisite for hearing it.

You cannot diagnose a hive from a distance. You have to be there — fully there, unhurried, with your attention organized around what's actually happening rather than what you expected to find. The moment you walk in already knowing what you're going to see, you stop being a beekeeper and start being a person confirming a story you already told yourself.

Leadership works the same way.

Presence is not physical proximity. It's attentional honesty — the discipline of being in the room you're actually in, with the people who are actually there, engaged with what is actually happening. Not managing an agenda. Not performing competence. Not waiting for your turn to speak.

Actually listening. Actually here.

> *"As a leader, you determine the vibe. Your decisions influence the tribe. Being intentional helps the hive."*

The Practice of Mindful Leadership

Leadership at its most reactive is just stimulus and response. Something happens, you react. Someone says something, you answer. A problem arrives, you solve it. Repeat, indefinitely, until you've spent an entire career without ever asking whether your responses were serving the work or just the urgency of the moment.

Mindfulness is the pause between the stimulus and the response. It is the moment — however brief — where you choose how to show up rather than simply defaulting to your patterns. Over time, practiced deliberately, that pause becomes a leadership posture: one where clarity, intention, and the actual needs of the situation can inform your decision rather than just your history or your anxiety.

This is not a wellness conversation. This is a performance conversation.

The most effective leaders I've observed — and the moments when I've led most effectively myself — share a common quality: they don't appear to be hurried even when the situation is urgent. They listen in a way that makes people feel fully received. They respond in a way that suggests they heard not just the words but the concern underneath the words.

That quality is not personality. It is practice.

A Personal Story: Leadership Through Reflection and Gratitude

There was a period early in my leadership when I was doing everything right and getting almost nothing right.

The strategies were sound. The hours were long. The commitment was genuine. But I was leading from a place of depletion — and depletion has a particular quality that's hard to see from the inside. Everything feels important. Everything feels urgent. The space between one thing and the next disappears. And the cumulative effect is a leader who is technically present but actually absent — going through the motions of engagement while the internal resources that make engagement real are running dry.

One morning, I sat down to reflect on the previous day and realized I had no memory of a single genuine exchange. I had been in meetings. I had sent messages. I had made decisions. But I had not actually connected with a single person I was supposed to be leading.

That stopped me.

I began a practice I've maintained since: every morning, before anything else, I write three things I'm grateful for and one intention for how I want to show up that day. Not what I want to accomplish. How I want to be.

It sounds small. It is not small.

What I found, over time, was that the practice reoriented my attention. The gratitude shifted my focus from what was wrong to what was working — not as denial, but as calibration. The intention gave me something to return to during the day when reactivity tried to pull me off course.

The effect on my leadership was measurable. I started listening differently. I began noticing things I had been moving too fast to see — the team member who was struggling but hadn't said so directly, the dynamic in a meeting that was signaling something important, the moment when someone needed acknowledgment before they needed direction.

Gratitude and presence are not soft concepts. They are operational tools. They changed what I was capable of seeing — and therefore what I was capable of responding to.

> The hive speaks constantly.
> But only the beekeeper who is still
> hears what it's actually saying.

Gratitude as Leadership Practice

Gratitude in leadership is not a feeling. It is a behavior.

It is the practice of naming — specifically and honestly — what is working, who is contributing, and what progress has been made that might otherwise go unacknowledged. In environments of chronic urgency, teams become invisible to themselves. They see only the gap between where they are and where they're supposed to be. Gratitude is the practice that makes the progress visible.

Here is what gratitude does for a team:

1. **It builds trust through being seen.**
   When people know that their contributions are noticed — not just during reviews but in the

ordinary moments of work — they trust that the environment is paying attention. That trust becomes the foundation for honesty and engagement.

2. **It shifts the energy of the room.**

    Urgency and anxiety are contagious. So is appreciation. A leader who begins meetings by naming what's working — specifically, not generically — changes the attentional orientation of everyone present before the agenda even begins.

3. **It reinforces what matters.**

    What you acknowledge, you amplify. When you express genuine gratitude for the behaviors you want to see more of — accountability, honesty, creative problem-solving, initiative — you are communicating your values more effectively than any policy statement.

4. **It sustains resilience.**

    Teams facing genuine difficulty need to be able to see that progress is real, even when it's incremental. Gratitude is how you make that progress visible — to yourself and to them.

Practical Steps for Mindful Leadership

1. **Start the day with intention, not urgency.**

    Before checking email, before the first message, take five minutes. Write three things you're grateful for. Set one intention for how you want to show up. Let those anchor you before the day's momentum takes over.

2. **Practice the listen-first principle.**

    In your next difficult conversation, commit to not offering your perspective until you've fully understood theirs. Not waiting to respond — actually listening to understand. Notice what you learn that you would have missed.

3. **Name the progress out loud.**

   Begin each team meeting with one acknowledgment — of a person, a behavior, a win. Make it specific. Not great job this week but I want to acknowledge how you handled that situation on Tuesday. Specific gratitude lands differently than generic praise.

4. **Pause before reacting.**

   When a charged moment arrives — a conflict, a failure, a challenging message — build in a deliberate pause before you respond. Even sixty seconds. That pause is where your intentional response lives, rather than your habitual reaction.

5. **Close the loop on what you noticed.**

   Mindfulness without expression has limited impact. When you notice something worth acknowledging — in yourself or someone else — say it. Write it. Don't let the awareness stay internal while the person who deserved to hear it never does.

Key Takeaways

1. **Presence is attentional honesty.**
   Being physically in the room is not the same as being present. Presence is the discipline of engaging with what's actually happening.

2. **Mindfulness is a pause, not a retreat.**
   The space between stimulus and response is where intentional leadership lives.

3. **Gratitude is operational.**
   It builds trust, shifts energy, reinforces values, and sustains resilience — not as side effects, but as direct outputs.

4. **Small practices compound.**
   A five-minute morning reflection, practiced daily, changes what you're capable of seeing — and therefore leading.

Your Challenge

This week, choose one practice from this chapter and commit to it every day for seven days:

- → The morning reflection: three gratitudes, one intention.
- → The listen-first principle in one conversation per day.
- → One specific acknowledgment in every team meeting.

At the end of the week, ask yourself: What did I notice that I would have missed without this practice?

The hive speaks constantly. Go still enough to hear it.

CHAPTER 8
Legacy and Impact of the Hive
Build Leaders. Leave Something That Lasts.

FROM THE HIVE

A queen bee does not live forever.

Her role — her essential, irreplaceable role — is to ensure that when she's gone, the hive continues. She doesn't accomplish this through dominance or indispensability. She accomplishes it by being the kind of presence that enables the colony to develop the capacity to survive without her.

Before she dies or departs, the hive prepares. Queen cells are built. New queens are raised. The colony doesn't collapse into her absence — it was never dependent on her in that way. Her legacy was never herself. It was the system she sustained.

I think about that often.

Not with morbidity, but with clarity. Because the question of legacy is ultimately the question of what kind of leader you chose to be — not in the highlight moments, but in the accumulation of ordinary decisions about how you invested your time, your attention, and your trust in the people around you.

Legacy is not built at the end. It's built now. Every day. In the choices you make about what to hold and what to hand off.

> *"True leadership is measured not by what you achieve, but by the leaders you develop and the impact you leave behind."*

Leadership Beyond Yourself

The leaders who leave lasting legacies share a particular quality: they are genuinely more interested in the growth of others than in the confirmation of their own competence.

This sounds straightforward. It is not easy.

It requires the discipline to give real responsibility to people who might not execute it the way you would — and to resist the urge to take it back when they don't. It requires the patience to develop someone slowly, to invest time that has no immediate return in deliverables or metrics. It requires an honest reckoning with ego: the recognition that being needed is not the same as being effective, and that a team's dependence on you is not a sign of your success but of a system's fragility.

Building leaders — real ones, not just capable executors — means creating the conditions where people can grow into authority, not just responsibility. It means letting them make decisions you could make better, so they develop the judgment that makes them capable of making better decisions on their own. It means being more interested in their development than in the short-term perfection of the outcome.

That is what builds a legacy. Not what you accomplished. What they were able to accomplish after you were gone.

A Personal Story: Building Leaders, Not Followers

I remember the moment the measure of my leadership shifted for me.

I was in an organization undergoing significant change — the kind of transition that surfaces every unresolved tension in a system, that makes visible all the things that were quietly broken beneath the functional surface. And in the middle of it, I looked around at the people I was leading and realized something that should have been obvious but hit me with the force of something newly discovered:

My job was not to get us through the transition.

My job was to build a team that could get through the next one — without me.

That reorientation changed how I spent my time. I stopped optimizing for my own effectiveness and started investing in theirs. I identified team members who had been overlooked — not because they lacked ability but because they lacked opportunity or visibility. People who had the capacity for more but had never been given the conditions to discover it.

I gave them real responsibility. Not the performance of it — actual decision-making authority over things that mattered. I supported them through the moments when that authority felt too large and resisted the temptation to step in when the struggle was productive.

I mentored in the spaces between the work — in the informal conversations, the post-meeting debrief, the moment after someone had done something worth discussing and we had a few minutes to examine what had just happened. I made the learning explicit.

I built systems that would hold after I left — documented processes, clear ownership, a rhythm of continuous improvement that didn't require my presence to sustain itself.

The most meaningful moment came months after I had moved on. Someone from that team reached out to tell me about a challenge they had navigated — not because they wanted my input, but because they wanted me to know they had handled it. Alone. Well.

That is the legacy I was building.

Not a program or a system or a metric.

> A person.
> Capable.
> Leading.
> On their own.

The Three Pillars of Legacy Leadership

1. **Develop Future Leaders — Invest Before It's Urgent.**

   Legacy is built through patient, sustained investment in people's development. Not just high-performers — the overlooked ones, the ones who needed someone to see what they were capable of before they saw it themselves. Identify them. Give them real responsibility, real authority, and real support. Mentorship is not a program. It is a posture.

2. **Build Sustainable Systems — Design for Your Absence.**

   The test of a system is not how well it functions when you're present. It's how well it functions when you're not. Document the knowledge that lives in your head. Create clear ownership structures. Build in feedback loops that don't require your initiation. Design for transition — not as an afterthought, but as a discipline practiced from the beginning.

3. **Lead With Purpose and Integrity — Let Your Values Shape the Culture.**

   The culture you leave behind is the accumulated effect of every decision you made about what mattered, what was tolerated, and what was celebrated. Values stated but not lived leave no legacy. Values lived consistently — especially when it was costly — become part of the culture's DNA. Lead in a way that makes your values visible in the behavior of the team, long after you've moved on.

The Ripple Effect of Legacy Leadership

Legacy expands in ways you cannot fully track.

The leaders you develop go on to develop others. The systems you build outlast multiple transitions. The culture you shaped influences decisions made by people who will never know your name but are working inside something you helped create.

This is not a small thing. This is the full measure of leadership. Not the quarter you closed or the initiative you launched or the recognition you received. The person who is leading somewhere right now because you gave them the conditions to become capable of it.

The queen does not build the hive. She enables the hive to build itself.

That is the legacy worth building.

Key Takeaways

1. Legacy is built in ordinary decisions.
Not in the highlight moments — in the daily choices about how you invest your time, trust, and attention.

2. Build leaders, not followers.
Develop people into authority, not just responsibility. Let them lead, even when it's imperfect.

3. Design for your absence.
A team that requires your constant presence is not a sustainable system. Build one that functions without you.

4. Your values are your legacy.
Not what you said you valued. What your decisions revealed you valued, consistently, over time.

Your Challenge

This week, ask yourself the legacy question:

Who am I developing — not utilizing, developing — right now?

- → Who on your team has potential you haven't fully invested in? What's one concrete way you could change that this week?
- → What knowledge or process lives only in your head that needs to be documented and transferred?
- → What decision could you hand to someone else — fully, with real authority — and protect the space for them to make it?

Don't wait for the transition to think about legacy. The transition is coming. Build now.

The queen's purpose is not the honey. It is the hive.

Conclusion:

> *"Leadership is not about standing above the hive — it's about working within it to inspire, influence, and build a legacy that endures."*

The Remarkable Hive

You've walked through eight principles now. Eight chapters, eight frameworks, eight invitations to examine your leadership from a different angle.

But the hive was never about the framework.

The hive is a living system. It doesn't succeed because the bees have studied the theory of collaboration or attended a workshop on resilience. It succeeds because every bee is fully committed to something larger than itself — and because that commitment is expressed not in intention but in action. Consistent, purposeful, unglamorous daily action.

That's the truth that none of the chapters could say directly, because it can only be understood through practice:

> Leadership is not what you know.
> It is what you do with what you know —
> and who you become in the process of doing it.

The eight principles in this book are not independent. They compound. Foundation makes accountability possible. Accountability makes collaboration real. Collaboration enables adaptability. Adaptability creates the conditions for innovation. Innovation, sustained over time, becomes sustainability. Sustainability, practiced with presence and mindfulness, produces legacy.

Pull on one thread and the whole system tightens. Neglect one and the whole system loosens.

Tend to all of them — imperfectly, consistently, with the willingness to ask hard questions and own honest answers — and you build something remarkable.

Reflect on Your Leadership Journey

Leadership is a journey without a final destination. There is no version of it where you arrive — where the foundation is fully set, the trust fully earned, the legacy fully built. There is only the next conversation, the next decision, the next moment where you choose whether to show up as the leader this situation requires.

The measure isn't perfection. It's direction and honesty.

As you move forward, carry these questions with you:

> → How am I showing up as a leader today — not in the big moments, in the ordinary ones?
> → Who am I developing, and am I investing enough to make that development real?
> → What am I building that will still be standing after I've moved on?

These are not questions you answer once. They are questions you return to — at the start of each week, each role, each season of your leadership.

Lead With Gratitude

Gratitude is the thread that runs through everything in this book.

Not gratitude as a feeling — as a practice. The practice of naming what is working, who is contributing, what progress has been made that might otherwise go unacknowledged. The practice of receiving difficulty without losing sight of what it's teaching. The practice of appreciating the people who make the work possible — not just when things go well, but especially when they don't.

Lead with gratitude and you will lead with presence. Lead with presence and you will lead with intention. Lead with intention and you will leave something behind worth leaving.

The Future of Your Hive

Every leader has the capacity to build something that outlasts them.

Not because of position or title or talent — but because of what they chose to do with the time and influence they were given. The leaders who build remarkable hives are the ones who stopped leading for credit and started leading for impact. Who measured their success not by what they achieved but by what they enabled.

The hive is remarkable not because of any single bee. It's remarkable because of the harmony that exists within it — the clarity of purpose, the depth of collaboration, the resilience that comes from every member understanding that their contribution is load-bearing.

Build that. In your team, your organization, your community.

Set the tone. Tend the foundation. Develop the people. Build the systems. Stay present. Lead with gratitude.

And go build something remarkable.

With gratitude,
Louis

About the Author

Louis G. Spence-Smith is a beekeeper, public sector technology executive, nonprofit founder, and the voice behind The Remarkable Hive. With over two decades of leadership across federal, state, and local government — including healthcare IT modernization, enterprise system transformations, and multi-agency governance — he brings both the strategic rigor of a systems thinker and the grounded perspective of someone who has done the work from the inside.

Louis is the founder of The Remarkable Hive, a platform built around the belief that sustainable, intentional leadership can transform organizations and communities. He is also the author of 21 Days of Gratitude and Your Remarkable Life, and his writing spans the intersection of leadership, mindfulness, and purposeful living.

When he is not writing or leading, Louis tends his beehives — where, he will tell you, the most honest lessons about leadership still happen.

Connect with Louis:
Website: www.theremarkablehive.org
Email: info@theremarkablehive.org
Instagram: @TheRemarkableHive |
YouTube: @AllThingsRemarkable

Notes